What Happens at an Orchard?

Perform Multi-Digit Arithmetic

Amelia Letts

NEW YORK

Published in 2015 by The Rosen Publishing Group, Inc.
29 East 21st Street, New York, NY 10010

Book Design: Katelyn Londino

Photo Credits: Cover Sura Nualpradid/Shutterstock.com; pp. 3–24 (background) jesadaphorn/Shutterstock.com;
p. 5 michaeljung/Shutterstock.com; p. 7 Jorg Hackemann/Shutterstock.com; p. 9 Dariush M/Shutterstock.com;
p. 11 Kletr/Shutterstock.com; p. 13 Jaroslaw2313/Shutterstock.com; p. 15 chloe7992/Shutterstock.com;
p. 17 (pomegranates in boxes) Fotokon/Shutterstock.com; p. 17 (pomegranate tree) MarkMirror/Shutterstock.com;
p. 19 (pecan tree orchard) Lindasj22/Shutterstock.com; p. 19 (pecans close up) IrinaK/Shutterstock.com;
p. 21 Peter Gudella/Shutterstock.com; p. 22 cabania/Shutterstock.com.

Library of Congress Cataloging-in-Publication Data

Letts, Amelia, author.
 What happens at an orchard? : perform multi-digit arithmetic / Amelia Letts.
     pages cm. — (Math masters. Numbers and operations and fractions)
 Includes index.
ISBN 978-1-4777-4933-3 (pbk.)
ISBN 978-1-4777-4934-0 (6-pack)
ISBN 978-1-4777-6456-5 (library binding)
1. Arithmetic—Juvenile literature. 2. Orchards—Juvenile literature. I. Title.
 QA115.L467 2015
 513.2—dc23
                                        2014004963

Manufactured in the United States of America

CPSIA Compliance Information: Batch #WS15RC: For further information contact Rosen Publishing, New York, New York at 1-800-237-9932.

Contents

A Place for Fruit

Do you like fruit? What about nuts or maple syrup? All these foods come from trees. Some families have fruit trees in their backyard or as part of a garden. However, when there are many trees that produce food in one place, it's called an orchard.

An orchard is a big area of land used for growing fruit and nut trees. Orchard owners sell their food to grocery stores and markets. Some orchards let people come and pick their own fruit.

It's fun to pick your own fruit at an orchard. It helps you understand where food comes from and how it grows.

Orchards produce a lot of food. You can think of a large number as being made of groups of 10. That's a two-digit number. It has a tens place and a ones place.

If you've ever added and subtracted **multiples** of ten, you know that only the tens place changes. That's because there are 0 ones, so the ones place stays at 0. It's the same when you multiply—the tens place increases, but the ones place stays the same.

It's easy to multiply a one-digit number by a two-digit number. The first step is multiplying the one-digit number by the two-digit number's ones place. Then you multiply the one-digit number by the two-digit number's tens place. Now you have the answer!

$$\begin{array}{r} 10 \\ \times\ 2 \\ \hline 20 \end{array}$$

An Array of Trees

Orchard owners use many growing **techniques** to keep their trees healthy. Healthy trees produce the best fruit, so this is very important. The **layout** of an orchard is 1 kind of growing technique. An orchard's layout is decided before the trees are planted.

Some orchards have rows of trees that make a square. Other orchards have rows of trees that form a rectangle. The rows of trees look like the **arrays** you multiply in math class.

How many trees are in an orchard that has 5 rows of 10 trees? You can find this answer by multiplying 10 by 5. First, multiply 5 by 0 to make 0 ones. Then multiply 5 by 1 to make 5 tens. Together, that makes 50.

10
x 5
50

Apple Picking

Apple orchards are best to visit during fall. That's when apples are in season, or when the fruit is ripe and ready to be picked. New York and Washington are the 2 biggest apple-producing states.

You can pick as many apples as you want when you visit an apple orchard. If you fill 2 baskets with 20 apples each, how many apples did you pick? Multiply 20 by 2 to get the answer. You picked 40 apples.

Let's use place value to solve this equation. Multiplying the ones places of both numbers, 2 times 0, makes 0. Multiplying the ones place of the one-digit number by the tens place of the two-digit number, 2 times 2, makes 4 tens. That makes our answer 40.

20
x 2
___
40

Apples from the orchard can be used in many different ways. You can make pies, applesauce, or simply eat them as a snack. Apples are very healthy, so they're a good fruit to eat.

An apple orchard is a great place to get the fruit needed to make apple pies. You can plan on using 6 apples to make a pie. If you want to make 10 pies for a school party, how many apples should you pick at the orchard?

It takes 60 apples to make 10 pies. You can find this answer by multiplying 6 times 10 or 10 times 6. The order of the **factors** doesn't matter as long as you multiply the ones place first, then the tens place.

$$\begin{array}{r} 10 \\ \times\ 6 \\ \hline 60 \end{array}$$

$$\begin{array}{r} 6 \\ \times 10 \\ \hline 60 \end{array}$$

How Many Pear Trees?

Some orchards grow pear trees. There are many different kinds of pears. Imagine an orchard grows 4 kinds of pears. If there are 20 trees of each kind, how many pear trees are in this orchard?

Break this equation into smaller parts to make it easier. Multiplying 20 by 4 is similar to multiplying 2 by 4, which is 8. Then, multiply 8 by 10 to make 80. There are 80 pear trees at this orchard.

You can also solve this by multiplying 4 times 10 first, then multiplying that **product** by 2. No matter how you group the numbers, they all make the same answer.

$(2 \times 4) \times 10 = 80$
$8 \times 10 = 80$

$(4 \times 10) \times 2 = 80$
$40 \times 2 = 80$

From the Orchard to You

Pomegranates are another fruit that grows on trees. Pomegranates are mostly grown in California. If you don't live in this state, you can't pick them yourself. So, how do pomegranates get from the orchard to you?

Orchard owners pick the best pomegranates off the trees. Then, they ship them around the United States. If an orchard fills 8 boxes with 90 pomegranates each, how many pomegranates do they ship? They ship 720.

Notice that 720 is a multiple of 10, just like 90. Multiplying a multiple of 10 makes a product that is also a multiple of 10.

$$\begin{array}{r} 90 \\ \times\ \ 8 \\ \hline 720 \end{array}$$

Some orchards grow nut trees in addition to their fruit trees. Almonds, pecans, and chestnuts all grow on trees. Nuts are a yummy and healthy snack.

If an orchard grows 7 different kinds of nut trees and there are 60 of each kind of tree, how many total nut trees grow at the orchard? Break this equation into 6 times 7, and then multiply that answer by 10. Multiplying 6 times 7 makes 42. Multiplying 42 by 10 makes 420. That's a lot of nut trees!

People eat nuts raw or roasted.
People also use them when they cook food and desserts.

60
x 7
420

(6 x 7) x 10 = 420
42 x 10 = 420

pecans

19

Selling Jam

Orchard owners don't like to waste anything they grow. If they don't sell all their food, they think of other ways to use it. Many orchards use the leftover fruit to make tasty jellies and jams.

Imagine an orchard makes 50 jars of raspberry jam. If they sell them for $1.00 each, how much money do they make? Multiply the money in the same way you'd multiply a regular whole number. Multiplying 50 times 1 is 50, or $50.00.

One rule of multiplication is that the product of any number multiplied by 1 is that same number. The total amount you get from selling each jar for $1.00 equals the number of jars the orchard had to begin with. What if each jar cost $2.00?

$$
\begin{array}{r}
50 \\
\times\ 1 \\
\hline
50
\end{array}
$$

Support Your Orchard

Picking fruit from an orchard is fun, but it's also a good way to help a business in your area. If you buy fruit from an orchard, it helps the orchard owners make money and keep their business open. When a business in your area makes money, it helps the whole community to be successful.

There are many kinds of foods to learn about, taste, and buy at orchards around the country. What kinds of orchard foods are you most interested in seeing?

Glossary

array (uh-RAY) An arrangement of something in rows and columns.

factor (FAK-tuhr) A number multiplied in a multiplication equation.

layout (LAY-owt) The way in which the parts of something are arranged.

multiple (MUHL-tuh-puhl) The number found by multiplying one number by another.

pomegranate (PAH-muh-gra-nuht) A fruit with reddish outer skin and seeds covered with sweet, red flesh.

product (PRAH-duhkt) The answer in a multiplication equation.

technique (tehk-NEEK) The way of carrying out a particular task.

Index

Due to the changing nature of Internet links, The Rosen Publishing Group, Inc., has developed an online list of websites related to the subject of this book. This site is updated regularly. Please use this link to access the list: www.powerkidslinks.com/mm/nof/orch